FLY AWAY HOME

©1996 COLUMBIA PICTURES INDUSTRIES INC. PHOTO BY TAKASHI SEIDA

Like the birds of the sky, God takes care of all living things. God gives us freedom and is with us in our grief.

PHENOMENON

Youth don't have to see strange lights to do spectacular things. Through faith, anything is possible!

© TOUCHSTONE PICTURES. PHOTO BY ZADE ROSENTHAL

DANCES WITH WOLVES

©1990 ORION PICTURES CORP. PHOTO BY BEN GLASS

Experience the risks and challenges along the trail of our Christian journey.

Behind the Scenes

Skip Parvin loves the movies, youth, and writing. Imagine how he feels being co-editor of Reel to Real! Skip wrote the programs for *Twister* and *Fly Away Home*. He is pastor at Tuskawilla United Methodist Church in Casselberry, Florida.

Mild-mannered **Ed McNulty** is a power-house champion of movies for spiritual insight. In addition to his regular editions of *Visual Parables,* he's now co-editor of Reel to Real. Ed contributed the *Les Miserables* devotion and the program for *Gandhi*. He is pastor of Bovina Presbyterian Church in Bovina Center, New York.

The youth at Boys Town High School, Father Flanagan's Boys Home, think that **Kathy Sorenson's** religion classes are the best—especially when she shows them God through the movies. Kathy, who lives in Omaha, Nebraska, is the Religion Department Chairperson at Boys Town. She wrote the program for *Dances With Wolves*.

Word about **David Stewart's** *Forrest Gump* retreats has spread almost as fast as Forrest runs. However, David's still waiting for his invitation to the White House! David is youth director at First United Methodist Church in Sevierville, Tennessee.

Among **Mike Lewis'** phenomenal achievements are his work with youth in the Florida Conference of the United Methodist Church and his writing about *Phenomenon* in this issue of Reel to Real. Mike lives in Orlando and attends St. Luke's United Methodist Church.

Les Miserables
(1935)

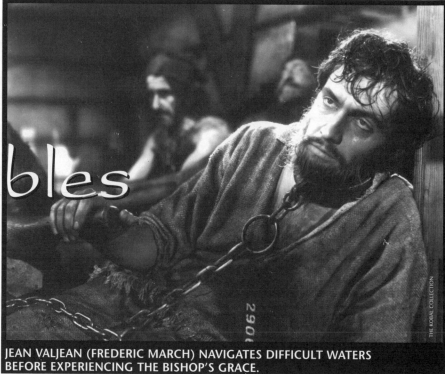

JEAN VALJEAN (FREDERIC MARCH) NAVIGATES DIFFICULT WATERS BEFORE EXPERIENCING THE BISHOP'S GRACE.

Our God, you bless everyone whose sins you forgive and wipe away.

Psalm 32:1

"Love your enemies, and be good to everyone who hates you. Ask God to bless anyone who curses you, and pray for everyone who is cruel to you. If someone slaps you on one cheek, don't stop that person from slapping you on the other cheek. If someone wants to take your coat, don't try to keep back your shirt. Give to everyone who asks and don't ask people to return what they have taken from you. Treat others just as you want to be treated."

Luke 6:27-31

Then the ones who pleased the Lord will ask, "When did we give you something to eat or drink? When did we welcome you as a stranger or give you clothes to wear or visit you while you were sick or in jail?" The king will answer, "Whenever you did it for any of my people, no matter how unimportant they seemed, you did it for me."

Matthew 25:37-40

SYNOPSIS

Jean Valjean, hero of the excellent 1935 film version of Victor Hugo's novel *Les Miserables*, could well join in the psalmist's plaintive cry, "How shall we sing the Lord's song in a foreign land?" The Frenchman is cruelly torn from his family and home for many years when he is caught stealing a loaf of bread to feed his starving sister and her children. While serving his sentence of many long years of back-breaking toil as an oarsman in a galley, Jean is reduced to the level of a brute by the sadistic cruelty of the guards. "The Lord's song" within him is displaced by his screams of agony and despair and the bitterness of the injustice of it all. Released at last, he can find no work or shelter because of his yellow ex-convict's passport. Every door is shut in his face until one stormy night when he is directed to the home of the local bishop.

FOR REFLECTION

- With whom in the story do you identify: Jean Valjean or the bishop? Or maybe the suspicious servant-woman or the gendarmes?
- When and where have we seen such grace in the lives of others? When and where have others seen such grace flowing through us? What are those moments in our relationship with others that could be turning points, turning disease and brokenness into health and wholeness?
- Can you think of a time when you were the recipient (or the conveyer) of such grace? What did you expect from your wrongdoing or shortcoming?
- How did you feel when you did not receive what you deserved? Is that not what grace is—the difference between what we deserve and what we receive at such moments?
- Why do such actions as the bishop's have a profound impact on the recipient (compared to a sermon or words of advice)? Is it partly because the action shows that the bishop is on Valjean's side?
- How can this story help you deal with others who wrong you?
- On whom have you given up as being too far gone to ever change? What do the stories in Luke and the film suggest you should do?

Against the wishes of the housekeeper, the clergyman invites Jean in. When the suspicious servant sets out their old dinnerware, the bishop orders their best silver plates to be used. The bishop treats Jean to a fine meal as if the unkempt guest were a person of high rank. Jean is taken aback by such unexpected treatment; but nevertheless, during the night the ex-convict sneaks off with a bag stuffed with the bishop's silver plates.

Jean is caught by the gendarmes the next day and is brought back to face the bishop. The bishop addresses Jean: "Come here, Jean. I'm very happy to see you again, Jean, because you forgot to take away the two silver candlesticks I gave you. They're worth at least two hundred francs. How did you come to leave them behind?"

The old bishop asks the gendarmes, "Didn't he tell you that the good priest with whom he spent the night gave him all this silver?" The chief officer replies that Jean did but that, of course, they had not believed him. The bishop says, "The silver is his. Give him his knapsack and passport."

"Life is to give, not take."
Les Miserables

The two policemen leave, and the puzzled Jean asks if he is really free to go. The bishop muses aloud whether anyone is really free. And as the bishop hands the two silver candlesticks to Jean, he dismisses his new friend with the admonition to remember that "life is to give, not take." They are words that the former convict will never forget.

When Jean leaves the bishop's house, he pauses at a roadside shrine to pray, obviously beginning the long journey of transformation. At that moment he feels at the core of his being the joy expressed by the writer of Psalm 32, "Our God, you bless everyone whose sins you forgive and wipe away."

We can never tell what effect our words or unexpected act of kindness will have on another person. It might be difficult to see Christ "in the least of these," especially if that person is as unkempt-looking as Jean Valjean or if that person has injured or threatened us. But the story of the bishop's kindness and Luke's story of Jesus and the thief on the cross remind us that when we become channels of God's grace, nothing is impossible. Like the crucified thief, the seemingly depraved Jean Valjean received grace at the time of his greatest need, thanks to an old clergyman who valued a human life far more than he did his silver dinnerware. The bishop took a risk. Some might call him foolish, perhaps, even aiding and abetting a known criminal. However, the bishop, like the Lord whom he emulated, saw in the wretched man brought back by the police not a depraved criminal but a child of God. That child of God, he thought, was well worth risking for, even to the point of telling a lie for him and seemingly throwing away his best silver pieces.

TEN COMMANDMENTS
OF USING REEL TO REAL

Welcome to REEL TO REAL: MAKING THE MOST OF THE MOVIES WITH YOUTH! The writers, editors, and design team of this youth resource hope that you enjoy the movies as much as we do. And make no mistake, your youth are enjoying and paying attention to the movies. Their gusto for the big (and little) screen presents a perfect opportunity to relate the life, lessons, and Good News of Jesus Christ in a current, meaningful, and fun way.

Christian movie lovers have always enjoyed analyzing and discussing religious themes on film. Without a doubt, filmmakers love to incorporate these images and themes. That's why REEL TO REAL is such a helpful and exciting addition to your youth ministry.

Here are some hints for incorporating the Christian images of film in your youths' lives. In fact, they are the Ten Commandments of using REEL TO REAL.

1. Thou shalt always preview the entire film before showing it to thy youth group.
2. Thou shalt always get parental consent before viewing questionable movies (see the Student Movie Pass on the inside back cover).
3. Likewise, thou shalt keep parents well informed of goings-on at all times. Honor thy fathers, mothers, and legal guardians!
4. Thou shalt never infringe upon the Federal Copyright Act (read The Fine Print on page 32).
5. Thou shalt remember—and remind skeptics in thy congregation—that a movie doesn't necessarily have to be a Christian movie to carry Christian messages and themes. Likewise, not all "religious movies" offer Christian messages and themes for thy youth.
6. Thou shalt not think that printed answers to session questions are set in stone. Sometimes there are no right or wrong answers, but oftentimes REEL TO REAL will furnish helpful responses in case the group gets stuck.
7. Thou shalt customize sessions and activities to the personality of thy youth group.
8. Thou shalt use the Video Viewing form to help thou quickly fast forward to selected movie clips. Boredom is not fun!
9. Thou shalt always preview the entire film before showing it to thy youth group. (OK, we realize that this is the first commandment, but it's *really* important.)
10. Thou shalt have a good time while learning the Good News of Jesus Christ.

Twister

One or Two Sessions

> "Go out and stand on the mountain,"
> the LORD replied. "I want you to see me
> when I pass by." All at once, a strong wind
> shook the mountain and shattered the rocks.
> *But the LORD was not in the wind.*
> Next, there was an earthquake,
> but the LORD was not in the earthquake.
> Then there was a fire, but the LORD was not
> in the fire. Finally, there was a gentle breeze.
>
> 1 Kings 19:11-12, emphasis added

THEME Our God is a God of love who does not wrathfully punish us through natural disasters such as tornadoes.

PURPOSE Youth will explore God's relationship to the natural world and will better understand how God relates to us.

BACKGROUND *Twister* is 114 minutes long and is rated PG-13.

CAUTIONS While the special effects are violent and occasionally frightening, the filmmaker has taken great pains to provide the power and intensity of the storms without gore. One brutal death occurs near the end of the film, but it too is filmed for intensity rather than gore. The special effects that create the tornadoes are spectacular. Please preview the entire film and send copies of the Student Movie Pass (parent consent form) on the inside back cover before you use this session.

MATERIALS

- *Twister* video
- Optional: *The Wizard of Oz* video
- VCR and TV
- Twister® games (the one with the colorful spots)
- Enough Bibles for the whole group
- Concordance(s)
- Library books, posters, or other references that show how tornadoes are formed and that have exciting pictures of actual tornadoes

SYNOPSIS

A team of scientists chase tornadoes in the hope of placing scientific equipment into the heart of a funnel cloud to learn how to predict the possible paths of tornadoes in the future. An old romance is rekindled between the leaders of the ragtag team as they compete with a highly financed corporate team.

BEFORE THE SESSION

Make sure you have viewed the entire video before showing it to the youth. This session is based on viewing the video clips referenced in Video Viewing, on page 6. If you wish to view the entire film with your group, plan to devote one session to just watching the film.

Prior to this REEL TO REAL session, encourage the youth to consider the reference materials you have compiled about actual tornadoes.

ICEBREAKERS

Play the party game Twister® with several floor mats so that all of the youth can participate at once. Another possibility: Bring Chubbie Checkers' "The Twist," "Let's Twist Again," and "The Peppermint Twist," or the Beatles' "Twist and Shout," and teach the youth how to dance "The Twist."

DISCUSSING & LEARNING

Have the youth look up the words *whirlwind* and *whirlwinds* in a *Strong's Exhaustive Concordance of the Bible* (if you use another concordance, be sure that *whirlwind* is included in its listings). They will find several listings in the Old Testament, such as 2 Kings 2:1, 11 and Job 37:9, 38:1, 40:6. See also Proverbs, Psalms, Isaiah, Jeremiah, Ezekiel, Daniel, Hosea, Amos, Nahum, Habakkuk, and Zechariah. Most of these deal with the destructive power of the whirlwind or of God using the power of the whirlwind to destroy enemies of Israel or the unfaithful.

Question 1: What is the difference between the tornado in *The Wizard of Oz* and the tornadoes in *Twister*?

Answer 1: The tornado in *The Wizard of Oz* becomes fantasy, a part of Dorothy's dream. The only person who is killed is the Wicked Witch of the East, when Dorothy's house lands on her. The tornadoes in *Twister* are meant to simulate actual killer storms that leave a path of death and destruction.

Question 2: Have any of you ever seen a tornado or been in one?

Answer 2: Encourage discussion about tornadoes, hurricanes, and severe weather in general to personalize the discussion.

Question 3: Do you believe that a Level 5 tornado is "the finger of God"?

Answer 3: The youth should respond that it appears in the Old Testament that God used the whirlwind as a destructive force to punish the enemies of Israel and the disobedient. After a few minutes of discussion, read aloud the lead Scripture for this session (1 Kings 19:11-12). Emphasize the verse that states, "But the LORD was not in the wind."

EXPLANATION

Through Jesus of Nazareth, we have learned that our God is a God of love who does not punish innocent people through natural disasters.

VIDEO VIEWING Begin with an opening prayer. First view the sequence in *The Wizard of Oz*, in which Dorothy is swept up and transported to Oz. Next, show one or more of the tornadoes from *Twister*, being sure to show the scene where one of the team's members refers to a Level 5 tornado as "the finger of God." Then watch the final "monster" tornado.

Suggestion: Preview the film on the VCR that you will use with the session. Make note of these key scenes so you can fast forward during the session, using these approximate start–end times and your VCR counter.

Start–End	Event	Count
0:00–0:05	Jo's dad and the tornado	_____
0:29–0:34	The first chase	_____
0:40–0:44	Sidewinder, sisters, and flying cows	_____
0:58–1:03	Back build down the road	_____
1:10–1:14	Drive-in mayhem	_____
1:18–1:22	Wakita aftermath	_____
1:26–1:32	First Level 5 tornado sighting	_____
1:33–1:44	The "monster"	_____
FOR USE WITH *THE WIZARD OF OZ*.		
0:14–0:19	The tornado transports Dorothy to Oz.	_____

On Palm Sunday 1994 a tornado destroyed the Goshen United Methodist Church while worship was in session. Among those killed was Hannah Catherine Clem, the four-year-old daughter of the church's pastor, Kelly Clem. Kelly's husband, Dale, is also a United Methodist pastor. All total, twenty parishioners died at the church or in related storms. The parsonage was destroyed as well. How can we believe that the destruction caused by these storms is God's intention?

PHOTO COURTESY C.A. SKINNER

Everything that was created received its light from him, and his life gave light to everyone. The light keeps shining in the dark, and darkness has never put it out.

John 1:3-5

God created the material universe to function according to certain natural laws, which are necessary for the physical world to exist. Tornadoes are one of the possible outcomes of the interaction of these natural laws. Stress how God is working through scientists to better predict the paths of these killer storms in order to prevent some of the suffering. Restate the Scripture, emphasizing that God is not "in the wind."

ACTION POINT Offer the youth a variety of ways to be in ministry to the victims of a natural disaster. This could range from going to a disaster area on a work team mission, to holding a fund raiser for relief efforts focused on a disaster area, to gathering needed items to ship to a disaster area.

Fly Away Home

One to Three
Sessions

© 1996 COLUMBIA PICTURES INDUSTRIES INC. PHOTO BY TAKASHI SEIDA.

"Look at the birds of the sky!
They don't plant or harvest. They don't
even store grain in barns. Yet your Father
in heaven takes care of them.
Aren't you worth more than birds?"

Matthew 6:26

THEME God gives us freedom, but with that freedom comes responsibility.

PURPOSE Youth will explore Christ's message of freedom, Christ's words for people who are dealing with grief, and his promise of hope.

BACKGROUND Fly Away Home is 107 minutes long and is rated PG.

CAUTIONS With the exception of three four-letter words, a joke about alcohol, and the live-in relationship of Amy's father with his love interest (mentioned but no live-in scenes), Fly Away Home is a good family movie.

MATERIALS
- Fly Away Home video
- VCR and TV
- Library books, posters, or other references that show wild geese in flight (Father Goose, by William Lishman, the book on which the movie is based, has many beautiful photographs.)
- Optional: Supplies for the Make a Goose activity on page 10

SYNOPSIS

After Amy survives an automobile accident in which her mother is killed, she goes to live with her eccentric artist/inventor dad in Canada. As the two begin to work at re-establishing their relationship, they find little common ground until Amy discovers several wild Canadian goose eggs and decides to secretly hatch them. The geese imprint on Amy, believing that she is their mother. As the geese grow, it becomes clear that they must be taught to fly and migrate. Amy's dad, who builds his own ultralight aircraft, teaches Amy to fly so that they might lead the geese to a winter home. In the process, Amy and her dad learn how much they love and need each other. The flight scenes in this film make it one of the most enthralling visual experiences ever filmed.

BEFORE THE SESSION

Prior to this REEL TO REAL session, encourage the youth to consider the reference materials you have compiled about wild geese.

USING THESE SESSIONS AND ACTIVITIES

These sessions and activities could be expanded to fit a number of formats. The film could be used in a short or long retreat or as an individual program. *Fly Away Home* is especially well suited for an intergenerational event. (A REEL TO REAL editor saw the film with his sons, four and eight years old, and they were both mesmerized.) This presents the opportunity for the youth to lead the church family in doing something together. The program presented here could be modified for children and adults. The program could be expanded to offer one session on each of the Scriptures (freedom, grief, and hope). These sessions are based on viewing the whole film before discussion, so one session must be devoted to just watching the film.

VIDEO VIEWING

Begin with an opening prayer. Then view *Fly Away Home*. If you've decided to view clips, use the Video Viewing chart below.

Suggestion: Preview the film on the VCR that you will use with the session. Make note of these key scenes so you can fast forward during the session, using these approximate start-end times and your VCR counter.

Start-End	Event	Count
0:08–0:10	Dad's crash	_____
0:13–0:14	Lunar lander model	_____
0:20–0:23	Amy's egg rescue	_____
0:29–0:30	Dad's fear that Amy is lost	_____
0:34–0:35	Geese imprint	_____
0:35–0:37	Attempt to clip wings	_____
0:48–0:50	Amy knows geese must go	_____
0:54–0:56	The breakout and air force	_____
1:15–1:22	Amy's crash	_____
1:26–1:28	The talk about Amy's mom	_____
1:31–1:33	Dad's crash during journey	_____
1:39–1:43	Safe arrival	_____

SESSION 1: FREEDOM

Christ has set us free!
Galatians 5:1

(All of Galatians 5 can be used in this discussion.)

THEME We are free to choose —free to choose to follow Jesus.

DISCUSSING & LEARNING

Question 1: Amy's dad built the lunar lander model because he always follows his heart. Should we always follow our heart?

Answer 1: Most of the time following our heart is a good thing. Sometimes it can lead us to be self-ish as Amy's father was selfish in that he allowed Amy and her mother to slip away because he would not compromise.

Question 2: Have you ever wanted to do something crazy like Amy's dad did? Do we sometimes need to do something crazy?

Answer 2: (personal opinion)

Question 3: Amy's geese think that she is their mother and imprint on her. How is that like our relationship with Jesus?

Answer 3: We are to pattern our lives after Jesus and try to be more Christlike each and every day. This is what discipleship is all about, learning what Jesus would have us do and becoming more like him.

Question 4: Why is Amy so freaked out when the wildlife officer tries to clip the wings of her geese? Would the geese be truly free if they could not migrate?

Answer 4: She knows that they wouldn't be truly free if they couldn't fly, and she comes to realize that they must migrate (leave her) to be free as well.

Question 5: When Amy and her dad break the geese out of the locked cages and land on the air force base, they are breaking the law. Do we sometimes have to do things that seem wrong for a greater good?

Answer 5: God expects us to follow the Holy Spirit and occasionally that might mean that we seem to be doing the wrong thing for the right reasons. God would not want us to break any laws unless an extremely important spiritual principle was involved.

© 1996 COLUMBIA PICTURES INDUSTRIES INC. PHOTO BY TAKASHI SEIDA.

SESSION 2: GRIEF

"I won't leave you like an orphan. I will come back to you. In a little while the people of this world won't be able to see me, but you will see me. And because I live, you will live. Then you will know that I am one with the Father. You will know that you are one with me, and I am one with you. If you love me, you will do what I have said, and my Father will love you. I will also love you and show you what I am like."

John 14:18-21

THEME Even in a time of heartbreak, grief, and loss, God is with us.

DISCUSSING & LEARNING

Question 1: How do you think Amy feels when she first sees her dad fly and then sees his crash landing?

Answer 1: Amy is at once amazed and frightened by flight. When he crashes, she is frightened that she has lost her dad.

Question 2: How do you think Amy's dad feels when he witnesses her crash?

Answer 2: He realizes how much he loves her; and he is afraid that he has lost her again, this time forever.

Question 3: When Amy's dad crashes on their flight south, what does Amy learn?

Answer 3: Amy says, "I can't find my way without you." But her dad helps her realize that even though she deeply loves her dad, she must find her own way in the world. Read aloud John 14:18-21. (Jesus is talking to the disciples.) Do you think that the disciples felt the same way Amy did? Jesus says that he will send the Holy Spirit to guide us.

"Hope is the thing with feathers."
Emily Dickinson

SESSION 3: HOPE

Faith makes us sure of what we hope for and gives us proof of what we cannot see.
Hebrews 11:1

And this hope is what saves us. But if we already have what we hope for, there is no need to keep on hoping. However, we hope for something we have not yet seen, and we patiently wait for it.
Romans 8:24-25

THEME Christ offers hope for all who need it.

DISCUSSING & LEARNING

Question 1: What do the eggs mean to Amy?

Answer 1: They give her something to hope for. Read aloud Hebrews 11:1.

Question 2: What else gives Amy hope?

Answer 2: The geese themselves give Amy hope after they hatch and as she watches them grow up. Other sources of hope are her dad's idea to lead the geese home and his confidence that she can do it. The town through which she flies to reach her final destination is called New Hope. Read aloud Romans 8:25. Point out the ways in which raising the geese, learning to fly, and leading them require a patient hope.

Question 3: Read aloud Romans 8:24-25. How does hope "save us"?

Answer 3: Hope saves us by helping us focus on the potential good in creation. When we are depressed and tempted to despair, as Amy was when she lost her mother, we can lose sight of the fact that God's love is working to redeem all of creation. As Christians, we hope for the good we cannot see in the physical world.

Question 4: Would you have had enough confidence in yourself to do what Amy did?

Answer 4: (personal opinion)

Question 5: What gives you hope?

Answer 5: (personal opinion)

Close in prayer or by completing "Make a Goose" on page 10.

Make a Goose

1. Make an exact square from origami or typing paper. (The square should be at least 8½ inches square.)
2. Fold the square in half to form a rectangle. Unfold it and repeat in the other direction, making sure that the ridges of these crosswise folds are on the same side of the paper.
3. Turn the paper so that the ridges of the fold are facing up. Fold the paper diagonally. Unfold that fold; and fold it diagonally in the other direction, making sure that the ridges of the diagonal folds are on the opposite side of the paper from the crosswise folds (see Figure a).
4. Holding the paper so that the crosswise ridges are facing up and one of the points is facing you, push the corners inward so that both crosswise folds and two of the diagonal folds refold. The result will be a square with the intersection of all the folds at one corner (Corner A) and the most open edges at the opposite corner (Corner D). The other corners, the ones that are alike, will be Corners B and C (see Figures b and c).
5. Fold one of the two-ply layers of Corners B and C in toward the center so that the raw edges of the paper line up along the crease that runs between Corners A and D (see Figure d). Flip the square over and fold the other layer of Corners B and C in the same manner. The result will look like a kite. Fold Corner A, the top of the kite shape, toward the folds you just made (see Figure e).
6. Unfold the folds you made in Step 5 (see Figures f and g). Pull one layer of Corner D up, refolding along the creases from the folds in Step 5 (see Figures g and h). Turn the paper over and repeat. The result will be a diamond shape with "legs" at Corner D (see Figure i). Fold the "legs" in half on both sides, making four folds (see Figure j).
7. Pull the "legs" up and into Sides B and C, having the "legs" stick out a little to the outside (see Figures k and l). These "legs" will form the head and neck and the tail of the goose.
8. Blow air in the hole at the base of the bird while gently pulling the wings toward the sides. Make the head by reverse folding one end of the head and neck portion as desired. Flatten and mold the beak area (see Figure m).
9. Fold the tail in half toward the base of the goose so that the tail is shorter and square (see Figure n).
10. After the geese are created, gather the group in prayer. Allow youth a moment to offer prayer concerns for themselves, their friends and family, and for the world. Ask youth to write their prayer concerns on the wings of their geese; and at the count of three, sail the geese and shout, "Lord, hear our prayers. Amen."

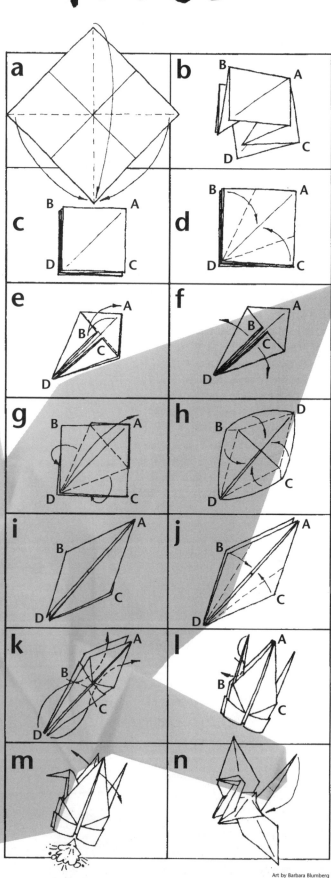

Art by Barbara Blumberg

The Sequel:

MORE GROUP ACTIVITIES AND RESOURCES FOR LEARNING

- **Origami** (the Japanese art of folded paper): Purchase a copy of *Flying Bird Origami,* by Yoshihide Momotani. This book contains instructions for 27 origami birds that will actually fly, including Wild Goose A and B. Have the group fold birds, fly them, and place them on the altar when you worship together.

- **Paper Airplanes:** Purchase a copy of the *The Ultimate Paper Airplane,* by Richard Kline, or *Best Ever Paper Airplanes,* by Norman Schmidt. The *Ultimate Paper Airplane* includes seven versions of the most successful paper airplane design of all time, which sets records for both distance and height. *Best Ever Paper Airplanes* includes 17 paper airplane designs and tips on decorating and flying them. Yes, one is appropriately named "The Goose."

- **Kites:** Purchase or build kites and fly them. Group kite building is a process that will help the youth work as a team. Books that will help include *The Big Book of Kites,* by Jim Rowlands, St. Martin's Press; *Kiteworks: Explorations in Kite Building and Flying,* by Maxwell Eden, Sterling Publishing Company, Inc.; *Kites That Really Fly,* by Troll, Troll Communications L.L.C.; *Making Kites,* by David Jefferis, Larousse Kingfisher Chambers, Inc.; *How to Fly a Kite: A Kiteflyer's Manual,* by Miller S. Makey, American Kiteflyer's Association; *Flying Kites,* by Baker Book Sales, Inc.

- **Frisbees:** Books like *Frisbee: A Practitioner's Manual and Definitive Treatise,* by Stancil D. Johnson, give you a wealth of possibilities for activities involving a Frisbee both indoors and out.

- **Balsa Wood Airplanes:** Remember the balsa wood kits for gliders and planes with rubber band motors? They're still out there. Buy more than enough plane kits for your entire group (always buy more in anticipation of guests and crash landings). Have the youth build and fly them. You can even set up competitions for longest flight, best stunt, coolest decoration, and others.

- **Wide-Wing Polystyrene Gliders:** These can be purchased at almost any toy store. You will need a large space to fly these as they go a long, long way—with wingspans of two and three feet. When put together with care, they sometimes seem as if they will fly forever. Find a hill for even better results.

For The Birds

(Other Well Known "Bird" Movies)

Brewster McCloud (1970): A strange little movie by Robert Altman about a young man whose life ambition is to fly around the Astrodome on wings he has made.

Birdy (1984): Nicolas Cage finds Matthew Modine, his lifelong friend, schizophrenic and silent. Healing comes through flashbacks to their childhood in working-class Philadelphia and Modine's desire to be a bird and fly.

The Birds (1963): In Alfred Hitchcock's masterpiece of horror, all the birds get together to attack humankind for no apparent reason—a metaphor for the abiding and inexplicable presence of evil in the world.

Bird Man of Alcatraz (1962): A ruthlessly violent man, played by Burt Lancaster, is rehabilitated through raising birds on the island prison.

Jonathan Livingston Seagull (1973): Often criticized for its shallow storyline and theology, this movie nonetheless presents some beautiful cinematography from the "bird's-eye-view" camera.

PHENOMENON

Jesus and his disciples returned to the crowd. A man knelt in front of him and said, "Lord, have pity on my son! He has a bad case of epilepsy and often falls into a fire or into water. I brought him to your disciples, but none of them could heal him."

Jesus said, "You people are too stubborn to have any faith! How much longer must I be with you? Why do I have to put up with you? Bring the boy here." Then Jesus spoke sternly to the demon. It went out of the boy, and right then he was healed.

Later the disciples went to Jesus in private and asked him, "Why couldn't we force out the demon?"

Jesus replied: "It is because you don't have enough faith! But I can promise you this. If you had faith no larger than a mustard seed, you could tell this mountain to move from here to there. And it would. Everything would be possible for you."

Matthew 17:14-21,
(See also Mark 11:12-14, 20-26, Luke 17:5-6.)

THEME Through faith, we can do amazing things.

PURPOSE Youth will see that through faith—even as tiny as a mustard seed—they are able to do phenomenal things.

BACKGROUND

Phenomenon is 120 minutes long and is rated PG.

CAUTIONS

This film contains mild profanity and brief nudity, when a character gets mooned. (Nudity is not in the selected clips.) Sexual intercourse between two adults is implied. They wake up in bed together fully clothed (also not in the selected clips). Please preview the entire film before you use this program, and send home a Student Movie Pass (parent consent form on the inside back cover) if you think that it is necessary.

MATERIALS

- *Phenomenon* video
- TV and VCR
- Bible
- Lots of newspapers and magazines
- Paper and pens
- Optional: *Phenomenon* soundtrack

SYNOPSIS

An ordinary auto mechanic encounters a strange event that gives him miraculous mental powers.

BEFORE THE SESSION

Prior to this REEL TO REAL session, encourage the youth to be prepared to explain one amazing thing that each has accomplished in life.

USING THESE SESSIONS AND ACTIVITIES

The program presented here could be modified to be used with both youth and adults. This presents the opportunity for the youth to lead the church family in learning together.

ICEBREAKERS

Have each person write on paper the most amazing thing he or she has ever done. Collect the papers. Read each one to the group and see if they can guess who did each amazing thing.

VIDEO VIEWING

Begin with an opening prayer. Then view *Phenomenon*. If you've decided to view clips, use the Video Viewing chart below.

Suggestion: *Preview the film on the VCR that you will use with the session. Make note of these key scenes so you can fast forward during the session, using these approximate start–end times and your VCR counter.*

Start–End	Event	Count
0:10–0:12	George's strange event occurs.	_____
0:24–0:27	George wonders what is wrong with him.	_____
1:05–1:08	George takes an I.Q. test.	_____
1:25–1:29	George tries to explain his powers to the local townspeople.	_____
1:29–1:31	George finds out about his tumor.	_____
1:35–1:39	George discusses brain surgery.	_____
1:44–1:47	George talks about death.	_____
1:57–1:59	The town has changed.	_____

DISCUSSING & LEARNING

Question 1: Do we use our whole brain?

Answer 1: No. Many victims of brain damage through accidents or disease learn to compensate by using other parts of their brain. While it was once thought that the brain could be mapped into regions that control various biological processes (senses like speech, hearing, and smell), it is now known that the brain is much more complex. Some people who have damaged parts of their brain have been able to be retrained to use a different part of their brain. We all experience times when we do not use our brains to capacity. The phrases "I can't believe I did that!" and "Why didn't I think of that?" come to mind.

Question 2: Define faith. Do we use our whole faith? Discuss the instances when someone is not using this whole faith.

Answer 2: (personal opinion)

FOLLOW UP

How would your life be different if you used all or more of your faith? How would your youth group/home/school be different?

Read the Scripture and use the song "Dance With Life" from the movie or the *Phenomenon* soundtrack to focus a discussion on the relationship between faith and life (the song is played during the movie's closing credits).

LEARNING ACTIVITY A

Have the youth scan the newspapers or magazines and cut out an article that shows either faith or lack of faith. Have each person present an article and tell what difference faith has made or could have made in the situation.

LEARNING ACTIVITY B

Divide into small groups. Have each person complete the following sentence: "Something I think I could do, but have always been afraid to do is. . . ."

LEARNING ACTIVITY C

Divide the youth into small groups. Within each group, let each person take a turn being the focus of the rest of the group. The person who is the focus must sit quietly and listen while the rest of the group tells him or her what they think he or she could accomplish through faith.

THE POINT Perhaps we dream that some extraordinary event will happen to us and make us smarter, richer, more talented, and the like. As Christians, our faith should be an extraordinary experience. God will enable us to do marvelous things.

ACTION POINT

Challenge the youth to do something incredible this week.

CLOSING Close with a prayer. "Our God of miracles, wonder, and phenomenal works, remind us that you are with us daily through the power of the Holy Spirit. Be with us—our families, friends, and others—during tough times and during times when our faith is tested. And when we find ourselves weak and when our faith is no larger than a mustard seed, remind us that you are with us, and through you, we can accomplish amazing things. Amen."

As the youth leave, play "Dance With Life" again.

The RATINGS

These are the Ratings Board classifications for movies featured in REEL TO REAL.

G "General audiences—all ages admitted."
- contains nothing in theme, language, nudity and sex, or violence that would be offensive to parents whose young children see the film
- not necessarily a children's movie
- no drug use
- violence is at a minimum
- small portions of language may go beyond polite conversation but are considered common, everyday expressions

PG "Parental guidance is suggested. Some material may not be suitable for children."

- parents must inquire about the film before allowing children to attend
- may have some profanity and violence
- no drug use
- no explicit sex but may be an indication of sensuality
- brief nudity may appear, but anything more must be rated R

PG-13 "Parents strongly cautioned. Some material may be inappropriate for children under 13."
- may depict drug use
- may contain only one of the sexual expletives
- Ratings Board may vote for this rating if it feels that the rating more responsibly reflects the opinion of American parents

R "Restricted. Under 17 requires accompanying parent or adult guardian."
- contains some adult material—language, violence, nudity, sexuality, or other content
- explicit sex is not allowed, although nudity and lovemaking may be involved
- may depict drug use

It is not the policy of REEL TO REAL to feature R-rated movies. REEL TO REAL will recommend an R-rated movie only if the film deals with a subject matter that must be studied by youth. The filmmaker must also have treated the subject matter responsibly. Only appropriate scenes of an R-rated movie will be recommended.

Gandhi

© 1982 COLUMBIA PICTURES INDUSTRIES, INC. ALL RIGHTS RESERVED.

"God blesses those people who make peace. They will be called his children! . . . When someone slaps your right cheek, turn and let that person slap your other cheek."

Matthew 5:9, 39

THEME Christ calls us to be peacemakers, reflecting the love that God has for all humanity.

PURPOSE The purpose of the session is to open the participants up to Christ's call to break the cycle of violence by responding to enemies in a new way, the way of love and a spirit of reconciliation based on his willingness to go to the cross.

BACKGROUND *Gandhi* is 187 minutes long and is rated PG. It won 8 Academy Awards in 1982, including Best Picture and Best Actor (Ben Kingsley).

CAUTIONS Although there is no questionable language or sexuality in *Gandhi*, several scenes contain violence and brutality. The violence is not excessively graphic, but it strongly conveys the harshness of the British treatment of Gandhi and his followers. Please preview the entire film before you use this program and send home a Student Movie Pass (parent consent form on the inside back cover) if you think that it is necessary.

MATERIALS
- *Gandhi* video
- VCR and TV
- Bibles
- Books and reference material about Gandhi (see page 18)
- Copies of the discussion questions and Scripture passage references

SYNOPSIS

The film follows the public career of the Indian revolutionary from his early years as a lawyer in South Africa, where he first endures the humiliation of the prejudice of whites and develops his philosophy and tactics of non-violent resistance, to his return to India, where his reputation as a fearless champion of the oppressed has preceded him. After a period of readjustment to his own country, he becomes involved with the National Congress Party, slowly assuming leadership of its revolutionary activities. Over the years, he develops non-violence into a force more powerful than the British guns and clubs, eventually forcing them to leave India—not as enemies but as friends. Like Jesus, Gandhi gives his life for his principles of love and non-violence.

BEFORE THE SESSION

Hand out reference material about Gandhi. Keep an eye out during the week for current local and world events dealing with conflict—between individuals, groups of people, nations, and the like—that would make for engaging discussion during Icebreakers.

USING THE SESSION AND ACTIVITIES

If you want your group to study Jesus' ethics of non-violence, Richard Attenborough's *Gandhi* offers some golden opportunities, filled as it is with episodes from the life of the man who was inspired by the Sermon on the Mount to free a nation through non-violence. Important scenes of non-violence are linked with a Scripture passage. The full film could be shown at a retreat or as part of a multi-session study.

ICEBREAKERS

Ask the group to name examples of conflict that currently exists in the world. If the youth don't include them, be sure to mention conflict between nations, between religious groups, between political parties, between schoolmates and friends. For each example given, ask the group to briefly discuss how they think the conflict will be resolved.

As a wrap-up to the discussion, tell the group that they are going to see how two men—Jesus Christ and Gandhi—were like-minded in their non-violent resolution of conflict.

VIDEO VIEWING Begin with an opening prayer. Then view *Gandhi*. If you've decided to view clips, use the Video Viewing chart below.

Suggestion: Preview the film on the VCR that you will use with the session. Make note of these key scenes so you can fast forward during the session, using these approximate start–end times and your VCR counter.

Start–End	Event	Count
0:12–0:20	Gandhi defies South African police by burning his pass and confronts bigotry.	_____
1:59–2:08 (7 minutes into the second video)	The Salt March to the Sea	_____

"You must be the change you wish to see in the world."
Gandhi

THE SESSION

Begin by asking some of the following questions:

- How many of you have been involved in a fight or strong argument? How did it end? With blows or harsh, insulting words? If so, how did you feel afterward?
- How do you think the other person felt? If you lost, was the desire to get even strong? Would you rather the disagreement end with both sides feeling better—about themselves and the opponent?

- Where can you get help for settling disputes? From the movies? How do most movie characters resolve disagreements? Stallone, Schwarzeneggar, Steven Seagal, others? Note how many movies are based on the desire for revenge!

Give the following overview of the life of Gandhi, especially if you are not viewing the entire film:

Yes, almost every movie hero chooses violence to overcome an enemy—but there is one film that offers a different way. And its hero is not a made-up character, but a man who really lived and practiced non-violence—*satyagraha* he called it, from Hindu words meaning "soul force." His name was Mohandas K. Gandhi. His people loved him so much that they called him Mahatma Gandhi, which means "great or enlightened one." Born in 1869, Gandhi studied in London to become a lawyer but wound up as a great spiritual leader and rebel against the rule of India by Great Britain.

"Don't listen to friends when the Friend inside you says, 'Do this.'"
Gandhi

Nineteen centuries of bloody history separate the founder of Christianity from the founder of India's freedom from British rule. Though far apart in time and cultures, the two men who spoke the key Scripture for this session are close in spirit, united in their common belief that violence leads to the destruction of the soul. They believed that violence destroys both the aggressor and the victim and that self-sacrificing love offers a solution to the seemingly unending cycle of violence.

Gandhi, the 1982 Academy Award-winning film, is a fascinating survey of the life of this strange little man whose courage and willingness to experiment in ethics and politics made such a difference in the world. We will look at and talk about two scenes from the film and passages from the Bible that deal with violence and non-violence.

Gandhi took seriously Jesus' teaching in Matthew 5:6, 38-41 about peacemaking by turning the other cheek.

Jesus seeks to break the cycle of violence in which an injured party strikes back at his enemy when insulted. Not only is there the refusal to participate in violence, but Jesus adds the positive action of offering the other cheek, seemingly cooperating in the aggressor's hurtful action. Jesus follows this up by urging a different reaction to the hated Roman occupational law under which many of the men in his audience had suffered. The law required Jewish males to carry a Roman soldier's baggage for up to a mile when so ordered. Instead of enduring the humiliation grudgingly, with a long face and murderous oaths muttered under the breath, Jesus urges his hearers to go willingly, not one, but two miles. No doubt his hearers were puzzled, even angered by such surprising words, which seem to go against human nature and desire.

FILM SCENE Gandhi defies South African police by burning his pass, refusing to stop even when he is clubbed to the ground. He and the priest then discuss Christ while walking down the street and are forced to confront bigotry and hatred.

DISCUSSING & LEARNING

Question 1: What impressed you about this scene? What effect did it have on the watching crowd?

Answer 1: (personal opinion)

Question 2: What effect did it have on the policeman? What, in general, was his belief about Gandhi and Indians that caused him to do what he did?

Answer 2: That they were inferior and cowardly and did not deserve any respect or rights.

Question 3: How might he have felt afterward? Would his feelings have been different if Gandhi had stopped or begged for mercy? Or tried to fight back?

Answer 3: Have youth play these scenarios out and express their personal opinion.

Question 4: Who has used such public demonstrations in our country? What were their effect?

Answer 4: Martin Luther King, Jr., wrote in his book *Stride Toward Freedom* that he once thought Jesus' command applied only to conflicts between individuals but that it was impossible between hostile groups and nations. What do you think?

Question 5: If you hit someone, and he or she responds the way Jesus commanded, how might you

feel about your opponent? Even if you first thought the person was acting out of cowardice, what might happen to your feelings about yourself? about your opponent? What if the person continued to receive your blows without hitting back or pleading for mercy?

Answer 5: (personal opinion)

"The good man is the friend of all living things." Gandhi

Question 6: And if you were that Roman soldier ordering a person to carry your baggage and the person continues to carry it beyond the required one mile, how might that affect you? your perceptions of yourself? your perceptions of your enemy? What do we usually think of someone who won't slug back? "Coward," "yellow," or "chicken"?

Answer 6: Gandhi often made it a point to declare that non-violence was not for cowards. He would rather a person fight an enemy with violence than to retreat into cowardly inaction.

FILM SCENE One of Gandhi's greatest public demonstrations, his famous Salt March to the Sea, is wonderfully restaged in the film—if there is time, this could be shown. The British government made it illegal to obtain salt, a basic staple of life in a hot country such as India, from any other source than the government outlets. Gandhi, after sending a letter outlining his plans to the Viceroy, set out with 78 followers. Every village along the 240-mile route was jammed with well-wishers cheering them on. After 24 days, the band, growing to thousands, reached the sea, where Gandhi dramatically waded into the ocean, picked up a pinch of salt on the beach, held it high and invited others to follow him in breaking the

law. Millions of Indians followed Gandhi's example in disobeying the unjust law. Almost 100,000 of them were arrested and overflowed the jails.

Question 7: Do you think that such non-violent resistance is a good application of Jesus' Beatitudes? Why or why not?

Answer 7: Some have interpreted Jesus' teachings as meaning that his followers not participate in any way in any kind of political movement. Instead, Christians should withdraw and practice passive resistance if overtaken by an oppressor. Compare this to Gandhi's (and Martin Luther King, Jr.'s) way. (Note that Gandhi emphatically rejected the term "passive resistance," claiming that we should actively resist evil, hence his coining the word *satyagraha,* from *satya,* which means "truth or soul," and *agraha,* which means "firmness, force, or power."

CLOSING The session could conclude with a prayer for love and peace. The famous Prayer of St. Francis of Assisi would be appropriate.

Lord, make me an instrument of
    thy peace;
where there is hatred, let me sow
    love;
where there is injury, pardon;
where there is doubt, faith;
where there is despair, hope;
where there is darkness, light;
and where there is sadness, joy.

O Divine Master,
grant that I may not so much seek
to be consoled as to console;
to be understood, as to under-
    stand;
to be loved, as to love;
for it is in giving that we receive,
it is in pardoning that we are par-
    doned,
and it is in dying that we are born
    to eternal life.

The Sequel
MORE GROUP ACTIVITIES AND RESOURCES FOR LEARNING

- *The Life of Mahatma Gandhi,* by Louis Fischer (Harper & Row, 1983). This authoritative biography inspired Richard Attenborough's film.

- *Gandhi: A Pictorial Biography,* by Gerald Gold (New Market Press, 1983). Includes photos from Gandhi's life and comparable scenes from the movie.

- *Stride Toward Freedom,* by Martin Luther King, Jr. (Ballantine Books, 1960). In Chapter 6, "Pilgrimage to Non-Violence," Dr. King relates how he came to believe in the Jesus-Gandhi ethic of non-violence, and he describes its dynamics.

- *Gandhi: Satyagraha and Agape,* by Ed McNulty (Rental: $30 from *Visual Parables,* P.O. Box 26, Bovina Center, NY 13740. Telephone: 607-832-4278). A two-screen slide/tape presentation chronicling the life of Gandhi and how his teachings were adapted by Martin Luther King, Jr., for the American Civil Rights Movement. The 360 slides of scenes from Gandhi's life and from the film come in two Kodak carousel trays. Script, tape, and discussion guide are included.

Another good film on the theme is *The War,* starring Kevin Costner.

My friends, you were chosen to be free.
So don't use your freedom
as an excuse to do anything you want.
Use it as an opportunity
to serve each other with love.
All that the Law says can be summed up in the
command to love others
as much as you love yourself.

Galatians 5:13-14

(Continue reading through Galatians 5:15-23
for the qualities of life in the Spirit.)

Dances
WITH WOLVES
Two to Three Sessions

THEME
God gives us freedom, but with that freedom comes responsibility.

PURPOSE
Youth will gain a new understanding of their own spiritual growth after viewing it in the context of Native American tradition.

BACKGROUND
Dances With Wolves (1990) is 181 minutes and is rated PG-13. It won 7 Academy Awards, including Best Picture.

CAUTIONS
Contains violence in some scenes, specifically battle scenes between Civil War soldiers; between Sioux and Pawnee tribes; or between soldiers and Dunbar. There is some nudity in two very brief scenes—one is a back view of Dunbar after bathing; the other is a brief premarital love scene between Dunbar and Stands With a Fist. Please preview the entire film before you use this program and send home a Student Movie Pass (parent consent form on the inside back cover) if you think that it is necessary.

MATERIALS
For Theme 1:
- *Dances With Wolves* video
- TV and VCR
- For prayer table: Bible, candle, objects that symbolize journey (backpack, compass, map, hiking boots), objects that symbolize risk-taking (bungee cord, college catalog), Native American fabric
- Blindfolds
- Bibles
- Copies of questions for Discussing & Learning

For Theme 2:
- *Dances With Wolves* video
- TV and VCR
- Clay or modeling clay for each person
- Post a large sheet of paper entitled "Holiness Is . . ."
- Markers

SYNOPSIS
Dances With Wolves is the timeless story of a Civil War hero, Lt. John Dunbar, whose new post turns out to be an abandoned fort. Alone at this fort, Dunbar befriends a neighboring Sioux tribe. Slowly, both overcome mutual fear and distrust, and Dunbar becomes an accepted member of the tribe. This acceptance is not without problem, especially when American soldiers discover Dunbar and brand him a traitor.

USING THESE SESSIONS AND ACTIVITIES
If possible view the movie in its entirety. That may mean having a special youth group viewing of *Dances With Wolves* in preparation for the following sessions. If you are limited to 45- to 60-minute sessions, it will take two or more sessions to finish the movie.

ICEBREAKERS
Set up a prayer area and a video viewing and discussion area. If you are using a prayer table, cover it with fabric of Native American design. On the table, display a Bible, a candle, and any objects that symbolize risk- or journey-taking. For this session, put out different snacks, something the youth are not used to eating—again, to symbolize taking risks.

As you greet arriving youth, invite them to notice the prayer table and different snacks. Encourage them to guess what the displayed objects and different snacks symbolize. Once everyone has arrived and settled in, call the group together for prayer around the prayer table. Ask for a volunteer to read 1 Corinthians 2:6-9. Then pray aloud the O Great Spirit Prayer.

VIDEO VIEWING
View *Dances With Wolves*. If you've decided to view clips, use the Video Viewing chart on page 23. The Video Viewing chart also will come in handy if you choose to answer What's Wrong With This Picture? which is also on page 23.

THEME 1: RISKS AND CHALLENGES ON THE CHRISTIAN JOURNEY

OPENING PRAYER
For each session, prepare a space with a prayer table, candle, Bible, and symbols that would reflect a Native American theme. Invite the group to gather for prayer around the prayer table. Ask them to take a few moments to quiet themselves by observing the Native American symbols on the prayer table.

Read aloud Galatians 5:13-23. Then read aloud the following prayer.

O GREAT SPIRIT PRAYER
O Great Spirit, whose voice we hear in the wind and whose breath gives life to all the world, hear us. We are small and weak; we need your strength and wisdom. Let us walk in beauty. May our eyes ever behold the red and purple sunset. Make our hands respect the things you have made and our ears sharp to hear your voice. Make us wise so that we may understand the teachings of our people. Let us learn the lessons you have hidden in every leaf and rock. We seek strength, not to be greater than our brothers, but to fight our greatest enemy—ourselves. Make us always ready to

come to you with clean hands and straight eyes so that when life fades, as the fading sunset, our spirits may come to you without shame.

But it is just as the Scriptures say, "What God has planned for people who love him is more than eyes have seen or ears have heard. It has never even entered our minds!" God's Spirit has shown you everything. His Spirit finds out everything, even what is deep in the mind of God.

1 Corinthians 2:9-10

© 1990 ORION PICTURES CORP. PHOTOS BY BEN GLASS.

DISCUSSING & LEARNING

Spend 7–10 minutes completing this trust walk activity with your group in order to help youth begin to focus on this session's themes: risk-taking, facing challenges, trusting in God. Have youth pair up. One person will be blindfolded and the other mute. The mute person is to lead the blindfolded person on a short walk. Before beginning, remind youth of the need for safety and for them to take the activity seriously. Ask the youth to keep these things in mind while participating in this activity.

- How does it feel to be blind or mute?
- How did you communicate with your partner?
- What challenges or difficulties did you face while blind or mute?

After 5 minutes of the trust walk, call the group back together and discuss the questions above and these.

- Was this harder or easier than you thought? Why?
- What kinds of risks did you have to take to participate in this activity?
- What can you learn from this activity?

Use the previous discussion as a springboard for explaining the purpose of this session by saying something like, "You've just completed a trust walk. Why do you think it is called a trust walk?" (Wait for some responses such as "I had to trust my partner because I could not see." "I had to trust that my partner wouldn't lead me into a wall." "I had to trust that my blind partner would understand where to go and what to do by just following my actions.")

Add to their responses by saying: "It's called a trust walk because it involves both people trusting and both people walking or going somewhere together. A trust walk involves some risks as well. What can we learn from a trust walk?" (Again, allow for their responses.)

Then add: "The trust walk can also teach us a lot about our own spiritual journeys with and to God. Our spiritual journeys will include challenges, risks, and communicating with and trusting God under difficult circumstances. We recently viewed *Dances With Wolves*. Now

we will use segments of this movie to help us understand even more about this spiritual journey to and with God."

Show the first 11 minutes of the movie, during Dunbar risks his life on the battlefield. After viewing have youth write their answers to the following questions:

- What risks did Dunbar take in this segment of the movie?
- Why did he take these risks?
- What were the results of his risk-taking?
- As a Christian, what risks or challenges are you facing?

Show the scene where Dunbar pokes Timmins (the man who transports Dunbar to the fort) in order to awaken him.

- When it comes to moving forward on your Christian journey, are you like John Dunbar—looking for direction and eager to reach a new destination? Or are you like Timmins—needing to be poked and prodded into moving in the right direction? Why?

To summarize, say something like: "Our Christian journeys are much like John Dunbar's journey. Spiritual journeys involve taking risks, seeking direction, and facing unexpected challenges. On our Christian journey, we risk being laughed at or excluded by friends or family who don't understand our journey. We risk having to make tough choices such as doing what's right even when it's difficult. We need direction for our journey, just as Dunbar needed directions for his journey to the fort. We sometimes proceed eagerly on our journey as Dunbar did; and sometimes we have to be poked and prodded to move along the right path, like Timmins. We are called to make the best of this journey, trusting that God is traveling with us."

ACTION POINT
As a way to live out what we have learned, each youth is to interview a parent, pastor, or other adult about the following:

- What risks, challenges, or unexpected situations have you experienced on your Christian journey or faith?
- How did you handle it?
- What were the results?

CLOSING
Read together Psalm 23. Then close with a prayer.

THEME 2: THE TRAIL OF A TRUE HUMAN BEING

Love is more important than anything else. It is what ties everything completely together.

Colossians 3:14

Other Scriptures: Jeremiah 18:1-6, Galatians 6:1-10, Colossians 3:12-17, and Matthew 5:3-12

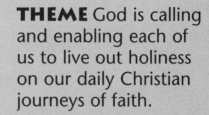

THEME God is calling and enabling each of us to live out holiness on our daily Christian journeys of faith.

OPENING ACTIVITY
Set up the VCR. Hang the large paper entitled "Holiness Is . . ." in a noticeable spot and put markers nearby. As youth arrive, greet them and invite them to notice the "Holiness Is . . ." paper. As they are munching on snacks and mingling, invite them to write on the paper what they think holiness is. Call the group together and discuss what has been written on the "Holiness Is . . ." paper.

DISCUSSING & LEARNING
Show the scene when Kicking Bird tells Dunbar that he is on the Trail of a True Human Being.

Question 1: What do you think Kicking Bird is talking about?

Answer 1: (personal opinion)

Question 2: What do you think Trail of a True Human Being is?

Answer 2: It is the path of holiness, living according to God's ways.

Question 3: Kicking Bird was the Sioux holy man. What qualities of Kicking Bird would you describe as holy? Why?

Answer 3: Patience, endurance, acceptance, generosity, wisdom, openness

Divide the group into pairs. Give each pair two of the Scripture passages and accompanying questions. Have the pairs answer the questions and then create a clay image that symbolizes holiness.

- Colossians 3:12-17. What are eight virtuous or holy attitudes or actions mentioned?

© 1990 ORION PICTURES CORP. PHOTOS BY BEN GLASS.

- Galatians 6:1-10. What are we to do or not do if our lives are directed by the Spirit?
- Matthew 5:3-12. What do you think this passage is saying about holiness?

ACTION POINT
Call the group together to discuss the following:

- What can we do as a group to be better examples of holiness for our families, school, church, local communities? (Generate a list of specific behaviors and actions.)

- Make a commitment as to which of the listed behaviors or actions your group will do.

CLOSING
Call the group to prayer. Have each pair describe their clay symbols of holiness. Read aloud Jeremiah 18:1-6 (see passage on right).

Pray aloud a brief prayer and close with the Lord's Prayer.

> The LORD told me, "Go to the pottery shop, and when you get there, I will tell you what to say to the people." I went there and saw the potter making clay pots on his pottery wheel. And whenever the clay would not take the shape he wanted, he would change his mind and form it into some other shape. Then the LORD told me to say: People of Israel, I, the LORD, have power over you, just as the potter has power over clay.
>
> Jeremiah 18:1-6

VIDEO VIEWING
If you've decided to view clips of *Dances With Wolves*, use the Video Viewing chart below.

Suggestion: Preview the film on the VCR that you will use with the session. Make note of these key scenes so you can fast forward during the session, using these approximate start–end times, and your VCR counter.

Start–End	Event	Count
0:00–0:11	Dunbar risks his life on the battlefield.	_____
0:20–0:22	Dunbar wakes Timmins.	_____
2:14–2:16	Trail of a True Human Being	_____

FOR USE WITH WHAT'S WRONG WITH THIS PICTURE? ON THE RIGHT

Start–End	Event	Count
0:23–0:25	Timmins has egg all over his face. Doesn't he?	_____
1:26–1:28	It takes one arrow to bring down a charging bison,	_____
0:32–0:34	and four to do away with Timmins. Wait! Is Timmins done away with?	_____
0:49–0:54	Stands With a Fist's designer rawhides and the layer-cut shag haircut that mysteriously changes length	_____
0:57–0:57	Dunbar says, "Hi!"	_____
2:34–2:36	A wild wolf with a choke collar?	_____

What's Wrong With This Picture?

- **Timmins (Robert Pastorelli) is Dunbar's (Kevin Costner) wagon driver on the trip to the abandoned fort. Timmins takes a bite of a pickled egg, only to spew it in all directions when Dunbar tells him to leave him alone at the fort. Some of the egg ends up on Timmins' mustache. Next shot, he looks at Dunbar and the egg has vanished. Another shot, it's back!**

- **How can the Native Americans bring down a charging bison with only one arrow, yet it takes four to do away with Timmins. And, if you watch closely, even after Timmins is clearly dead and even scalped, he takes a breath!**

- **Where does Stands With a Fist (Mary McDonnell) get all those designer rawhides?**

- **What's more, who is the Native American hairdresser who invented the layer-cut shag look just for her? Even better, why does her hair change length in the scene in which Dunbar first encounters her mourning the death of her husband?**

- **Why does Dunbar greet people with the modern expression "Hi"?**

- **Why would a dead wild wolf be wearing a choke collar?**

Native American Movie Quiz

Question 1: In what movie does an old Cherokee Indian played by Chief Dan George lament: "I myself never surrendered; but they got my horse, and it surrendered."

Answer 1: *The Outlaw Josey Wales* (1976)

Question 2: In what movie does Old Lodge Skins, a Cheyenne played by Chief Dan George, lament (again) to his adopted white grandson (Dustin Hoffman): "There is an endless supply of white men, but there has always been a limited number of human beings."

Answer 2: *Little Big Man* (1970)

Question 3: What movie has a tribal police officer (Graham Greene, a.k.a. Kicking Bird) pull over an FBI agent (Val Kilmer) for speeding, and when Kilmer asks to see the radar says, "I don't need no radar . . . I listened to the wind when you went by; it said, '59—Nail him.' "

Answer 3: *Thunderheart* (1992)

Question 4: In what obscure "Native American" movie did Graham Greene first attract critical attention as an exceptional actor with his portrayal of a Vietnam veteran?

Answer 4: *Powwow Highway* (1989)

Question 5: How many movies featuring the great Apache leader Geronimo have been made? A. 7, B. 12, C. 16, D. 27

Answer 5: C. 16—Actors who have played Geronimo include Jay Silverheels (a.k.a. Tonto), Chuck Conners (*The Rifleman*), Ian MacDonald, and Wes Studi.

Question 6: What award-winning documentary produced by Robert Redford and directed by Michael Apted examines an "incident" at South Dakota's Pine Ridge Reservation in which two FBI agents died?

Answer 6: *Incident at Oglala: The Leonard Peltier Story* (1992)

Question 7: What great Native American leader and statesman is immortalized in the movie *I Will Fight No More Forever*?

Answer 7: Chief Joseph of the Nez Perce

GUMPISM FOR DANCES WITH WOLVES:

"LIFE MUST HAVE BEEN A LOT SIMPLER WHEN THE INDIANS RAN THIS COUNTRY."

FROM *THE WIT AND WISDOM OF FORREST GUMP*, BY WINSTON GROOM.

FORREST GUMP
GUMP CAMP, THE RETREAT

For everything there is a season, and a time for every purpose under heaven.

Ecclesiastes 3:1, *NRSV*

The entire Scripture (Ecclesiastes 3:1-8) goes with the song "Turn, Turn" on the *Forrest Gump* soundtrack.

© 1994 BY PARAMOUNT PICTURES. PHOTO BY PHIL CARUSO.

THEME Forrest Gump asked simple questions and made simple yet truthful observations about the complexities of life. Likewise, Jesus Christ calls us to live the simple ideal of treating our neighbors as precious children of God.

PURPOSE Youth will focus on the moments Forrest was Christlike to his neighbors. The youth will be challenged to look for opportunities in which they can be Christlike for their neighbors as well.

GUMP CAMP ACTIVITIES

A retreat-full of Gump Camp activities are described here and on the next two pages.

GUMPARDY! Test the knowledge of the youth group's biggest Gump know-it-alls. Answers and questions are on page 30.

TOUCH FOOTBALL Weather permitting, hold the Shrimp Bowl of touch football. For a touchdown to count, the scoring team must shout, "Stop, Forrest, Stop!" And remember the team prayer.

ELVIS IMPERSONATION CONTEST Crank up music by the King and hold a competition for the best—or worst—impersonation. Thankyaverymuch.

BACKGROUND
Forrest Gump is 142 minutes long and is rated PG-13.

CAUTIONS
The movie contains profanity, pre-marital sex, a trip to a strip bar, hints of parental sexual abuse, and realistic war scenes. If you play the soundtrack during breaks, you may want to be selective about some of the songs. One lyric includes the line, "Everybody must get stoned." The movie is representative of changes that have occurred in American history. Please preview the entire film before you use this program and send home a Student Movie Pass (parent consent form on the inside back cover) if you think that it is necessary.

SYNOPSIS
Tom Hanks inspires viewers through his portrayal of "Forrest, Forrest Gump." The movie spans three decades of American history. Special effects put Forrest right in the middle of the action. He even gets to meet three presidents. Forrest

rises from a child with a disability to a football star, from a Vietnam hero to a multi-millionaire. He can be seen as a Christ figure throughout the movie. Forrest may not have been a smart man, but he knew what love was.

MATERIALS
- *Forrest Gump* video—for viewing and possibly as a prize for Gumpardy!, on page 30
- VCR and TV
- Nametags
- *Forrest Gump* soundtrack (to play during breaks)—This could also be used as a prize for Life Is Like Contest.
- Paper and markers for Life Is Like Contest
- Elvis music for the Elvis Impersonation Contest and Elvis T-shirts to use as prizes—one shirt for middle school and one for high school
- Table tennis table, balls, and paddles for the tournament. Don't forget a sign-up sheet for participants.
- Copies of Life Questions for small groups on page 29
- A box of chocolates to spring on the group during Discussing & Learning
- Forrest Gump-like food. Possibilities are popcorn shrimp; "Run, Forrest, Run" cake; Dr. Peppers® (also for the Dr. Pepper® Drinking Contest); cookout stuff; soft drinks and cookies for break times; popcorn for the movie; and the like. Good sources for Gump recipes are *Bubba Gump Shrimp Co. Cookbook: Recipes and Reflections from Forrest Gump* (ISBN 0-8487-1479-2) and *Forrest Gump: My Favorite Chocolate Recipes* (ISBN 0-8487-1487-3).
- For an in-town retreat, host families might provide breakfasts, but involve the youth in KP duty as a service and in helping with meals.
- Rooming list—Check with retreat center; some require this in advance.
- Football and different color shirts or flags that will help members identify their team for the Shrimp Bowl

BEFORE THE SESSION
Recruit adult helpers. Try to recruit one adult for every eight youth. Give these helpers specific instructions (or written guidelines). You may want to have a meeting prior to the retreat to discuss guidelines and expectations and to help ease volunteers' anxieties.

Room setup is essential! Some games require moveable sturdy chairs, and others require lots of room. Decide where small groups will meet.

LIFE IS LIKE CONTEST The winner is the person who best completes the sentence "Life is like. . . ." (Just as Forrest said, "Life is like a box of chocolates. You never know what you are going to get.") Ask, "Why do you say that?" It might be helpful to come up with a few beforehand in case the group needs a starter. Discuss the humor and seriousness of each answer.

LIFE QUESTIONS FROM FORREST GUMP Divide the group into small groups of no more than eight youth and a leader. Have each person draw a slip of paper with a question from the Life Questions page and discuss each question among the small group. After this session, collect each group's questions and reuse them at another small-group session later in the retreat.

THINGS TO REMEMBER WHEN ORGANIZING A RETREAT

- Set a registration deadline (3–4 weeks prior to the event). Count on last-minute add ons and drop outs. Always check the refund policies of the retreat center or hotel. If you are hosting an in-town retreat, prepare to have an extra house available to host youth in case a family emergency cancels a house already committed.
- When staying in a hotel, make sure that you check all rooms in advance for damage. Report damage to the front desk to save your damage deposit when you check out. When hosting an in-town retreat, make sure that the host families understand their responsibilities and give them guidelines for the retreat.
- Make sure that there is plenty of food. If the retreat is a theme event such as "Gump Camp," be creative. For instance, a cake with the words "Run, Forrest, Run" on it is a great touch. For other ideas and great recipes, see *Bubba Gump Shrimp Co. Cookbook: Recipes and Reflections from Forrest Gump* (ISBN 0-8487-1479-2) and *Forrest Gump: My Favorite Chocolate Recipes* (ISBN 0-8487-1487-3). Have a plan to pass leftover food on to a local mission or food pantry.
- Always leave retreat facilities cleaner than you found them. If you do, you will be warmly received when you visit again.

DISCUSSING & LEARNING

Join in an opening prayer. "Almighty God, remind us that you created each and every one of us in your image. And your image is diverse, complex, and interesting. We celebrate the differences in each of us which make us your unique children. Thank you for life and life abundant. In Jesus Christ we pray. Amen."

Use the following narrative to create your own youth talk. You may want a youth to lead the session.

Retard, loser, freak, gimp, stranger, redneck, Charles, druggie, alcoholic, cripple, stupid, different, stripper, baby killer, sinner. What is normal? And who gets to decide?

"Life is like a box of chocolates." It is sad that we rarely look for the beauty in one another. Much of our time is spent trying to cut one another down. We try to neatly categorize one another. We fail to see magnificent work of God in ourselves and others.

Forrest was called many names. However, he (like Jesus during his trial and crucifixion) never retaliated. Instead, Forrest always looked for the best in others. When the boys on the bus told Forrest that there was no room, he didn't yell at them. He simply kept looking for his place.

Answer these questions aloud or to yourselves:
- Whom do you know or see daily who acts like Forrest?
- How do you view this person? Describe him or her.
- How do you suppose God views this person?

Forrest saw Jenny as the beautiful love of his life. He was deeply committed to her although she seemed ungrateful.

Answer these questions aloud or to yourselves:
- Whom do you know who acts like Jenny?
- How do you view this person? Describe him or her.
- How do you suppose God views this person?

Forrest couldn't understand why people made such a big deal about African Americans wanting to go to

DR. PEPPER® DRINKING CONTEST
Line 'em up and knock 'em back. The winner of the 30-second contest might win a six-pack of Dr. Pepper®. Gee, thanks a lot!

TABLE TENNIS TOURNAMENT
Post sign-up sheets, make brackets, and paddle away! Give the winner a fast food gift certificate or some other clever prize.

POPCORN SHRIMP FEAST
Don't limit the soiree to popcorn shrimp. You can try your boiled shrimp, your barbecued shrimp, your shrimp kabob, or any other concoction you and your youth come up with. See Forrest Gump cookbook suggestions under Materials on page 26.

Answer these questions aloud or to yourselves:
• Whom do you know who has felt like Lt. Dan?
• How do you view this person? Describe him or her.
• How do you suppose God views this person?

When Forrest got rich, he shared his money with Bubba's mother; and even she asked him if he was crazy. Jesus himself had been referred to as "God's own fool." Forrest was classified a fool by the educational system. Jesus gave all he had to help others. Forrest risked his life to save his friends in the war. Jesus forgave those who killed him. Forrest continually forgave Jenny, who took advantage of his love.

Too often, we play the part of Jenny. We take advantage of God's love and grace. We do our own thing and look for love elsewhere. We are ungrateful, but God still loves us. Too often, we give up on others. We end relationships instead of trying to reconcile. We judge others as unworthy of our time and love. We do not forgive, and we do not forget.

Forrest offered chocolate to people he did not know, to people who did not want any, even to people who thought he was crazy. [Pass a box of chocolates around the group, if you have one.] God offers love to us even when we do not think we need it and when we do not deserve it. Was Forrest a real person? No, but the world sure needs people like him.

Watch the movie again. Look for times when Forrest does something Jesus might have done. Then pay close attention to your everyday life. Look for ways you can be Christlike to those with whom you come in contact. The world sure needs you.

school with whites at the University of Alabama. Instead of spitting on the black girl as she entered the building for her first day of class, he (a football star) helped her by returning a book she had dropped. Forrest grew to love Bubba, a black fellow soldier, who had an especially large lip and talked endlessly.

Answer these questions aloud or to yourselves:
• Whom do you know or see daily who acts like Forrest?
• How do you view this person? Describe him or her.
• How do you suppose God views this person?

Forrest saved several of his fellow soldiers, including Lt. Dan Taylor. Lt. Dan was unappreciative. Forrest had to remind him that even without legs that he was still Lt. Dan Taylor.

Photocopy the following questions. Then cut the copied questions apart into strips. Have members of small groups draw a question and read it to the group. Ask group members to respond.

- Forrest's mom said, "Don't let anyone tell you they are better than you." Who do you compare yourself with? Why? What happens when you feel that you do not measure up?

- What does *normal* mean?

- Forrest's mom slept with the principal to get Forrest into school. Why do you think she did that? How far do you think you would go to help someone you love a lot? What boundaries do you have for yourself in getting what you want?

- "God didn't make us all the same," Forrest's mom said. Why do you think we are so drawn to conformity?

- On Forrest's first day to ride the bus, he met Dorothy Harris. After introducing himself, he said, "We ain't strangers no more." Have you ever met a stranger and became instant friends? Why do you think that he or she was so easy to like?

- Jenny once prayed to become a bird to escape from her dad. What do you pray for most? Have you ever prayed to escape from someone or a certain situation? What did you do after praying?

- "A promise is a promise." How do you feel when you discover that someone has been dishonest with you? How hard is it to keep your promises?

- Forrest began to run amazingly fast while he was being chased. It was a miracle, according to his doctor. Have you ever had a miracle happen to you? If so, describe your miracle.

- When Forrest got on the bus for school, several people said, "Seat's taken!" Have you ever felt like there was no place for you? Describe the feeling and how you handle those times.

- Jenny and Forrest were "like peas and carrots." Who is your best friend and why?

- "Sometimes we do things that don't make sense." What do you do when life does not make sense? Who helps you deal with the inconsistencies?

- If shoes tell a lot about a person, what story would the pair you are wearing right now tell? Would they tell where you've been? Where you're going? Describe the happiest time in your life since owning your current pair of shoes. Describe the worst time. What would you like to see happen in your future?

- Do you ever wish you had said something to a friend or done something for a friend that you did not say or do?

- Forrest's mom told him that his dad was on vacation when he possibly had left them. Is it OK for parents to lie? In what circumstances might a lie be OK? How does this affect a Christian, when honesty is to be highly valued?

- One day Forrest and Jenny returned to the house where she grew up. She began to throw rocks at the house as she remembered her growing-up years. What do you think Forrest meant when he said, "Sometimes there just aren't enough rocks?" How would you rate your growing-up years on a scale of 1 to 10, with 10 being perfect? Why did you pick that number? If you could change one thing in your life history, what would you change?

- Forrest cut the local school football field grass for free. What job would you do for free?

- What do you think Forrest's mother meant when she said, "Life is like a box of chocolates"?

- What is the best gift you have ever received?

- Bubba had a big lip. Have you ever chosen not to be friends with someone because of the way he or she looked? Why do you think our society puts so much emphasis on physical appearance?

- Whom would miss you most if you moved away or were gone tomorrow?

- Forrest rescued Jenny from the nudie bar and Lt. Dan from the jungle. Neither was thankful. Have you ever helped someone only to find them ungrateful? Do you ever get tired of helping people?

- What similarities can you find between Forrest and Jesus?

- What expectations do you have to live up to? Who puts the most pressure on you?

- What scares you the most?

- What do you think your destiny is?

- Jenny told Forrest she had a virus (possibly AIDS) that doctors could not cure. He married her anyway because he loved her. Could you have done that?

- When Forrest got rich, he gave Bubba's mother Bubba's share. Would you have done this? Why or why not?

- Jenny asked Forrest what he wanted to be; and he responded, "Ain't I gonna be me?" What does it mean to be you?

- Forrest could run like the wind. Tell the group about one of your talents.

- Jenny once asked Forrest to pray with her. Do you have a friend with whom you can pray? How do you feel when someone tells you that he or she is praying for you?

GUMPARDY!
ANSWERS & QUESTIONS

Use these questions to see who remembers the most about the movie. Play a game similar to Jeopardy!® with three youth who feel that they are Gump gurus. Have them write down their answers and reveal them to the group. Give the winner a prize such as a box of chocolates or a copy of the movie. Remember that your response must be in the form of a question.

A The last name of Forrest's friend Jenny.
Q What is Curran?

A The full name of Forrest's friend Bubba.
Q What is Benjamin Buford Blue?

A Two things you can tell about a person by their shoes.
Q What is, "where they have been and where they are going"?

A Forrest and Jenny were like these tasty vegetables.
Q What are peas and carrots?

A The U.S. Army, including Forrest's troops, looked for Vietnamese soldiers they referred to by this common name.
Q Who is "Charlie"?

A Rain fell for this number of months while Forrest was in Vietnam.
Q What is four?

A The college football legend who coached Forrest at the University of Alabama.
Q Who is Paul "Bear" Bryant?

A The uniform number that Forrest wore at Alabama.
Q What is 44?

A The U.S. Army rank, held by Forrest, that is abbreviated P.F.C.
Q What is Private First Class?

A The Tennessee city where Jenny made her singing debut.
Q What is Memphis?

A Lt. Dan's last name.
Q What is Taylor?

A Forrest needed to catch this bus to get to Jenny's home in Montgomery.
Q What is Number 9?

A The bus driver who drove Forrest to school.
Q Who is Dorothy Harris?

A You'll wear these in your hair if you are going to San Francisco.
Q What are flowers?

A Lt. Dan's fiancee.
Q Who is Susan?

A It's how long Forrest ran in years, months, days, and hours.
Q What is 3 years, 2 months, 14 days, and 16 hours?

A Forrest could eat this many chocolates . . . or say he said.
Q What is 1½ million?

A A derogatory term for a person with a physical disability, it was Forrest's boyhood nickname.
Q What is "Gimp"?

A Greenbow County High School shared this mascot with a Major League baseball team in the South.
Q What is Braves?

A The deadly disease that Jenny contracted.
Q What is an unknown virus, possibly HIV/AIDS?

A The date Jenny died.
Q What is March 22, 1982?

A The blonde actress whose picture was in President Kennedy's bathroom.
Q Who is Marilyn Monroe?

TOM HANKS QUIZ

Tom Hanks hasn't always been Forrest Gump. See how many of these other Tom Hanks characters and movies you can identify.

Question 1: In what film do we hear a Tom Hanks' character give a deeply moving interpretation of the aria "La Mamma Morta" from the opera *Andrea Chenier*?

Answer 1: *Philadelphia* (1993), Andrew Beckett

Question 2: In what movie does a young boy make the wish "I want to be big" and then wakes up the next morning as an adult played by Tom Hanks?

Answer 2: *Big* (1988), Josh

Question 3: In what movie does Tom Hanks say to his partner, "It looks like you swallowed a tennis shoe and the laces are hangin' out"?

Answer 3: *Turner and Hooch* (1989), Scott Turner. He is speaking to his partner—a massive, ugly dog—about the drool dangling from his huge floppy jowls.

Question 4: In what movie does Tom Hanks say to his partner, "Wait a minute, Connie Swail? Don't you mean the virgin Connie Swail?"

Answer 4: *Dragnet* (1987), Pep Streebeck. He addresses the final one liner in the movie to his partner, Joe Friday (Dan Aykroyd).

Question 5: In what movie is the saddest line delivered by a Tom Hanks' character, "We just lost the moon"?

Answer 5: *Apollo 13* (1995), Jim Lovell

Question 6: In what movie does Tom Hanks' character give a geography lesson to his son by saying, "I'll show you a sign.

Here's a sign. Where is Seattle? Where is Baltimore?"

Answer 6: *Sleepless in Seattle* (1993), architect Sam Baldwin, who is destined to fall in love with Annie (Meg Ryan)

Question 7: In what movie does a woman with whom Tom Hanks' character has fallen in love say, "I love my husband," and he responds, "If we're going to get married, you'll have to get over that"?

Answer 7: *Punchline* (1988), bitter stand-up comic Steven Gold

Question 8: In what movie does Tom Hanks' character lament, "All my life I've been waiting for someone, and when I find her she's a fish"?

Answer 8: *Splash* (1984), Allen Bauer, who has fallen in love with a mermaid played by Darryl Hannah

Question 9: In what movie does Bruce Willis' character make the following comment about Tom Hanks' character and his own character: "This is Sherman, who started with so much, lost everything; but he gained his soul. Whereas I, you see, who started with so little, gained everything. But what does it profit a man if he gains the whole world and loses? Ah, well, there are compensations."

Answer 9: *The Bonfire of the Vanities* (1990), stockbroker Sherman McCoy (a reference to McCoy's decline after he is brought down by his lack of ethics in dealing with a hit-and-run accident)

Question 10: In what movie does Tom Hanks' character exclaim, "It's not that I can't help these people, it's just that I don't want to"?

Answer 10: *Volunteers* (1985), selfish preppie Lawrence Bourne III, who buys his way into the Peace Corps to escape his gambling debts but who is converted in the end

> "(Film is) an extension of childhood, where everybody wants to be freer, everybody wants to be powerful, everybody wants to be so overwhelmingly attractive. Or wants to have comradeship and be understood."
>
> Marlon Brando (*Rolling Stone;* May 20, 1976)

THE FINE PRINT

Q I understand that motion pictures are protected by federal copyright laws. Do these copyright laws apply to showing movies in our church youth group?

A Yes. Under the law, for-profit and nonprofit organizations are required to have a public performance license to show movies, which include purchased and rental videocassettes.

Q How does my church obtain rights to show full-length films and film clips for youth group and other Christian education purposes?

A You need to obtain a public performance license (sometimes called a site or umbrella license) to show movies on home video publicly, even for educational purposes. An umbrella license can be granted by The Motion Picture Licensing Corporation. The MPLC's Church Desk handles these requests. Contact Harald Bauer, Executive Vice President, at 800-515-8855 (fax 203-270-8830).

Q What is an umbrella license and what does it allow the church to do?

A An umbrella license is a 12-month license purchased by your church that enables you to use copyrighted films of your choice for preaching and teaching. If your church purchases an umbrella license, you may use entire videos or clips not only in your youth group with REEL TO REAL, but your pastor may use clips with sermons.

Q How much will an umbrella license cost?

A Generally, the umbrella license costs $95 for a 12-month period.

Q Are there any less expensive alternatives?

A Yes. Many denominations—through conferences, jurisdictions, dioceses, and other structures—already have public performance license agreements for their churches. Under these agreements, the church office negotiates with the MPLC a much lower rate per church. If your church's jurisdiction has an umbrella license for its churches, your church can qualify for the lower rate. If you're not sure, call your church's jurisdictional offices and ask whether an umbrella license agreement exists or is being pursued.

Q Without an umbrella license, are there ways to incorporate current film and REEL TO REAL in our youth group study?

A Yes. Oftentimes a movie featured in REEL TO REAL is still playing at the theaters or at the "dollar theater." So your group can pay admission price, see the movie during an outing, and discuss the REEL TO REAL session afterward or during another group time.

Another idea is to check out the Coming Attractions on the back cover of REEL TO REAL. Many of those movies are still playing in local theaters. You can make a youth outing of the movie and then discuss it when the next REEL TO REAL comes out.

Q Are there other restrictions, even if we purchase an umbrella license?

A Yes. You may only use pre-recorded videos, such as those purchased legally by an individual or rented from video stores or the public library.

You may not dub selected clips on another cassette to show to your group—the clip must be cued from the original pre-recorded tape. No license exists for showing movies taped from television or cable.

If you have any questions about your legal rights, call The Motion Picture Licensing Corporation at 800-515-8855.

THE COPYRIGHT LAW

- The Copyright Act grants to the copyright owner the exclusive right, among others, "to perform the copyrighted work publicly" (Section 106).

- The rental or purchase of a home videocassette does not carry with it the right "to perform the copyrighted work publicly" (Section 202).

- Home videocassettes may be shown, without a license, in the home to "a normal circle of family and its social acquaintances" (Section 101) because such showings are not "public."

- Home videocassettes may also be shown, without a license, in certain narrowly defined "face-to-face teaching activities" (Section 110.1) because the law makes a specific, limited exception for such showing. *There are no other exceptions.*

- All other showings of home videocassettes are illegal unless they have been authorized by license. Even "performances in 'semipublic' places such as clubs, lodges, factories, summer camps, and schools are 'public performances' subject to copyright control" (Senate Report No. 94-473, page 60; House Report No. 94-1476, page 64).

- Institutions, organizations, companies, or individuals wishing to engage in non-home showings of home videocassettes must secure licenses to do so—regardless of whether an admission or other fee is charged (Section 501). This legal requirement applies equally to profit-making organizations and nonprofit institutions (Senate Report No. 94-473, page 59; House Report No. 94-1476, page 62).